Contents

Introduction

What would you do if you had a bad headache? Maybe you would reach for an aspirin tablet. Some people might prefer to use **complementary** or **alternative medicine** (CAM). They may try **acupuncture** or **hypnotherapy**. A very few might even try much stranger cures, such as sleeping on a magnetic bed or drinking a cup of their own urine.

As this selection shows, it can be hard to put your finger on exactly what CAM is. The term lumps together hundreds of remedies, potions, treatments and therapies. Many have little in common with each other – except that they are different from the **orthodox** medical treatment usually provided by Western doctors and hospitals.

People in the USA now spend as much money on CAM as on orthodox medicine. In the UK there are 50,000 practitioners – twice as many as ordinary doctors. Many young people use CAM, especially those whose parents use it. The online bookstore Amazon stocks nearly 5,000 titles about alternative remedies. Many famous people swear by some form of CAM. Oscar-winning film star Halle Berry uses a lipstick containing the herb St John's Wort to combat depression.

Popular treatments

Why is CAM so popular? One reason may be that up to 50 per cent of people in rich, Western countries such as the USA now suffer from conditions such as high blood pressure, asthma or depression. These conditions cannot be completely cured by modern drugs. Millions of people around the world say they have got relief from CAM where **conventional medicine** has failed.

CAM sees illness as an imbalance in the patient's whole system. It tries to get to the underlying root cause of a health problem. The aim is to heal the person's mind, body and spirit rather than just his or her sore throat or stomach ache.

However, if it is not used properly CAM can sometimes do more harm than good. And with a bewildering range of pills, ointments, potions, teas and sprays on sale, it seems harder than ever to sort the good from the bad.

Need to Know

Alternative Medicine

Claire Wallerstein

Heinemann
LIBRARY

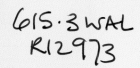

www.heinemann.co.uk/library

Visit our website to find out more information about **Heinemann Library** books.

To order:

 Phone 44 (0) 1865 888066

 Send a fax to 44 (0) 1865 314091

 Visit the Heinemann Bookshop at www.heinemann.co.uk/library to browse our catalogue and order online.

Produced by Roger Coote Publishing
Gissing's Farm, Fressingfield, Suffolk IP21 5SH, UK

First published in Great Britain by Heinemann Library, Halley Court, Jordan Hill, Oxford OX2 8EJ, part of Harcourt Education.
Heinemann is a registered trademark of Harcourt Education Ltd.

Editorial: Cath Senker
Design: Jamie Asher
Picture Research: Lynda Lines
Consultant: Wendy Miller, British Holistic Medical Association
Production: Viv Hichens

Originated by Ambassador Litho Ltd
Printed and bound in China by South China Printing Company

ISBN 0 431 09808 5
07 06 05 04 03
10 9 8 7 6 5 4 3 2 1

British Library Cataloguing in Publication Data
Wallerstein, Claire
  Alternative medicine. - (Need to Know)
  1.Alternative medicine - Juvenile literature
  I.Title
  615.5

Acknowledgements
The Publishers would like to thank the following for permission to reproduce photographs: Associated Press p. 27 (Elaine Thompson); Bristol Cancer Care Help Centre pp. 44, 45; Corbis Stockmarket p. 17 (Tom & Dee Ann McCarthy); FLPA p. 46 (Brandenburg); Sally and Richard Greenhill pp. 4–5, 7, 14; Hodder Wayland Picture Library pp. 28 (Bo Svane), 38; Hutchison *front cover (woman)* (J. Highet); pp. 15 (Nancy Durell McKenna), 23 (Tony Souter), 35 (John Burbank); Medipics p. 10 (Dan McCoy/Rawson); MPM Images *front cover (pills)* (Daniel Rogers); Oxford School of Reflexology p. 49; Science Photo Library *front cover (needles)* (Tek Image), pp. 6 (Maximilian Stock Ltd), 9 (Oscar Burriel), 11 (Jean-Loup Charmet), 16 (CC Studio), 18 (Geoff Tomkinson), 20 (Tek Image), 21 (Andrew McClenaghan), 25 (Françoise Sauze), 29 (Phil Jude), 32 (Cordelia Molloy), 33 (Paul Biddle & Tim Malyon), 43 (Simon Fraser/Searle Pharmaceuticals), 51 (Josh Sher); Still Pictures p. 47 (Mark Edwards); Topham pp. 5 (PA), 13 (Image Works), 19 (Chapman), 31 (PA), 37 (Image Works), 41 (Image Works).

Cover photograph of meditating woman reproduced with permission of Hutchison Library; acupuncture needles with permission of Science Photo Library; homeopathic medicine with permission of MPM Images.

Every effort has been made to contact copyright holders of any material reproduced in this book. Any omissions will be rectified in subsequent printings if notice is given to the publishers.

Any words appearing in the text in bold, **like this**, are explained in the Glossary.

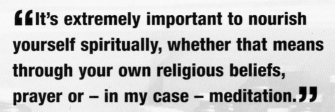

"It's extremely important to nourish yourself spiritually, whether that means through your own religious beliefs, prayer or – in my case – meditation."

(Australian actress and breast cancer sufferer Olivia Newton-John)

Glamorous film star Halle Berry is one of many celebrities who use alternative therapies.

Alternative medicine

CAM covers a wide range of healing therapies from all around the world. A few are now practised by ordinary doctors and are available in Western hospitals. However, many more remain outside the field of modern medicine and science, and have not been tested or proved in clinical trials.

Holistic treatments

Many CAM therapies are ancient, and nearly all involve a theory of **holistic treatment**. 'Holistic' comes from the Greek word 'whole'. It means that the whole person is being treated – his or her body, mind and spirit. For example, a doctor may simply prescribe tylenol/paracetamol and plenty of fluids and rest for a person with 'flu. A CAM practitioner, however, would try to deal with what caused the sickness in the first place. He or she would look at everything from the patient's diet and energy levels to any mental or emotional problems, such as stress or grief. By dealing with all of these, the aim would be to make the person stronger and more able to resist illness in the future.

Many alternative remedies are not actually what we often think of as 'medicines', used to cure a disease. A lot of people who use them have nothing wrong with them. They use CAM treatments such as vitamin supplements, **meditation** or **yoga** as a lifestyle treatment to keep healthy over the long term. They often use several CAM therapies at the same time.

A gentler alternative?

Many of today's man-made drugs are very strong and can have nasty **side effects**. CAM practitioners say their products are safer and gentler because they are natural.

However, natural does not necessarily mean safe or good. Snake venom, tobacco, arsenic and strychnine (used in rat poison) are all 'natural'. On the other hand, some **conventional medicines** are natural.

For example, aspirin is derived from willow bark and important cancer-fighting drugs come from the yew tree.

Some patients use CAM therapies as their only medical treatment. This is a real 'alternative' to conventional medicine. More often, however, CAM is used at the same time as conventional medicine – and is '**complementary**'. Many people feel that neither conventional nor **alternative medicine** has all the answers and so choose to combine the best aspects of both.

❝Alternative medicine is defined as that which cannot be tested, refuses to be tested, or consistently fails tests. If a healing technique is demonstrated to have curative properties in properly controlled trials, it ceases to be alternative. It simply becomes medicine.❞

(Biologist Richard Dawkins, of Oxford University, UK)

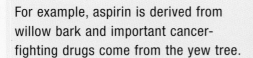

Some forms of alternative medicine may prove to cure or prevent common conditions such as 'flu, which cannot be cured by conventional medicine.

Alternative medicine

CAM therapies

Very broadly, CAM therapies can be broken down into the following categories.

- Alternative medical systems, for example, Traditional Chinese Medicine (TCM), and **Ayurveda** from India. According to these ancient systems, disease is caused by a disruption in the flow of energy around the body. They emphasize the importance of herbal remedies, diet and the power of the body to heal itself. Although Western scientists do not believe that our bodies have any invisible energy channels, both these medical systems have had a great deal of success. They are used by many millions of people, both in their Asian homelands and in the West.

- Mind-body systems, which include meditation and **hypnosis**. These send the mind into an altered state to harness its healing power. Scientists now agree that our minds have much more power over our physical health than we once thought. For example, meditation could raise the levels of important chemicals in our bodies that help to fight off infection.

- Biologically-based treatments. Many CAM products and therapies, for example **herbal medicine** and **homeopathy**, involve natural compounds believed to have medicinal properties. These range from plants and herbs such as ginseng or artichoke, to non-plant products such as royal jelly (from bees) or shark cartilage.

- Manipulative and body-based methods. Some examples are **osteopathy**, **chiropractic** and yoga. These involve bending and moving the body either to cure an illness or injury, or to keep it strong and healthy. The body can also be used to affect the mind. For example, **massage** can be extremely helpful in calming the minds of people who feel very stressed, depressed or nervous.

- Energy therapies. **Reiki** and faith healing, for example, claim to use the practitioner as a kind of channel to send good, healing energy into the patient. Others are said to use the energy of objects such as crystals to rebalance disrupted energy levels.

Yoga was developed thousands of years ago in India. It is used by many people to improve their general health. For example, the singer Madonna is a big fan of astanga yoga, which is very energetic and requires a lot of practice.

History

Today, Western doctors can carry out major life-saving operations such as heart transplants and brain surgery. It is hard to believe that medicine as we know it dates back only 100 years or so. Think of **antibiotics** – something we take for granted today. These were not produced until the mid-twentieth century. Until then, people often died of simple infections.

Our Stone Age ancestors developed the very first medicines many thousands of years ago. Through a long process of trial and error, they learnt that certain plants and substances could treat and cure some diseases. Even animals have learned to do this. For example, a dog will eat grass when it has an upset stomach.

Orthodox medicine

Traditional **herbal medicine** could not cure all diseases though. So in the Middle Ages, scientists in Europe started trying to develop new, stronger and more effective treatments. These were often based on experiments in laboratories – the beginning of today's **orthodox medicine**.

Trepanning (knocking a hole in the skull) was a common, but dangerous, treatment used in ancient times. It is still used today in some African countries in cases of bad headaches or mental illnesses.

However, the scientists' task was difficult. For many years it was illegal to dissect (cut open) dead people to find out about diseases or how the body worked. This meant they often had to rely on the old teachings of Ancient Greek and Roman scientists, some of which were very wrong. For example, they thought epilepsy sufferers were possessed by demons, and that the body was governed by four liquids or 'humours' – blood, phlegm, black bile and yellow bile.

This led to many treatments being used that were dangerous or only worked by accident – such as using leeches to suck sick people's blood. This process was called bleeding. Sometimes large amounts of blood were drained out of people, weakening or even killing them.

Wise women or witches?

In any case, most people could not afford to see a doctor. Some would see a barber surgeon, who could carry out operations such as pulling out rotten teeth and amputations (cutting off diseased limbs). Most relied on wise old women who remembered the ancient medicinal herbs and folk remedies. These form the basis of many of today's '**alternative**' therapies.

The Christian Church came to believe these women were witches, often because their treatments worked so well that they seemed to be using magic. In 1484 the Pope called for witch-hunting campaigns across Europe. From then until 1750, tens of thousands of women were burned to death. A lot of alternative medical knowledge was lost with them.

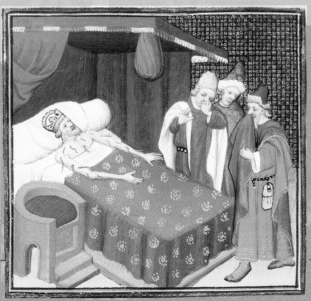

Hundreds of years ago, leeches were used to suck out the supposedly 'bad' blood of sick people.

Ancient traditions

In the rest of the world, medicines that are now called '**alternative**' were positively encouraged. **Acupuncture**, for example, was invented more than 4000 years ago in China. **Ayurveda**, still widely used in India, is 5000 years old. It is based on ancient religious texts. Rather like the Ancient Greek theory of humours, it says that three types of energy (*dosha*) control a person's personality, intelligence, strengths and weaknesses. Imbalances in this energy cause illness, and the dosha must be restored by means of **yoga**, a **detoxifying diet**, **massage** and herbs.

Massage was widely used in Ancient China, Greece and Rome. In the West, however, the Church came to frown on such intimate body contact. This means the healing power of massage has only been rediscovered in the West over the past 100 years or so.

CAM in the West

The first big development of new CAM therapies in the West did not happen until the 1800s. Systems such as **naturopathy** and **homeopathy** were partly developed to provide gentler alternatives to grisly 'scientific' treatments still being used, such as bleeding. Around the middle of the twentieth century, however, there was a string of great medical breakthroughs, which saved millions of lives. These included the development of **antibiotics** and the introduction of mass **immunization** campaigns.

While **conventional medicine** became very successful in some areas, it still could not cure common illnesses such as colds, depression or cancer. Conventional drugs could also have horrible long-term **side effects**. Disappointment with modern medicine in Western countries has led more and more people to look for answers in ancient and newly-developed alternative techniques. Today, CAM is more popular than ever.

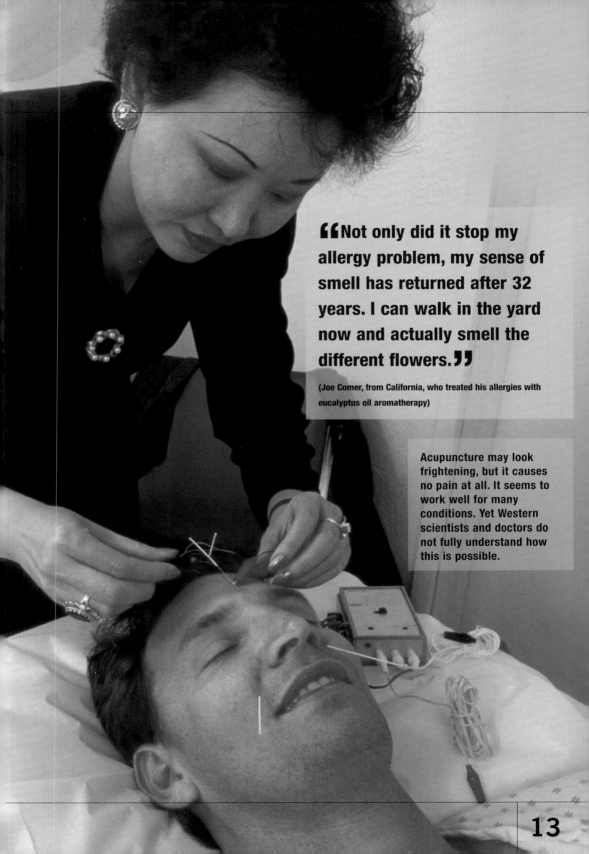

> **"Not only did it stop my allergy problem, my sense of smell has returned after 32 years. I can walk in the yard now and actually smell the different flowers."**
>
> (Joe Comer, from California, who treated his allergies with eucalyptus oil aromatherapy)

Acupuncture may look frightening, but it causes no pain at all. It seems to work well for many conditions. Yet Western scientists and doctors do not fully understand how this is possible.

Who uses what?

In the USA, more than $20 billion is spent on alternative remedies each year, a little more than on **conventional medicine**. More than 40 per cent of all Australians and Canadians use alternative remedies In the UK the figure is at least one in five.

The most frequent users in the West are white, middle-class, young to middle-aged, well-educated women. The most popular treatments are relaxation techniques, **herbal medicine**, **massage**, **chiropractic**, vitamins and **homeopathy**. **Hypnotherapy**, **acupuncture** and **osteopathy** are also popular. Spiritual healing is popular in Holland and **reflexology** in Denmark. In Germany doctors cannot qualify unless they complete courses in **alternative medicine**.

Medicine in poor countries

But for the 80 per cent of the world's population living in poor countries, and for indigenous (native) people in developed countries, CAM is not an 'alternative' choice. It is often the only option. India has an entire government ministry devoted to **Ayurvedic** medicine, while in Mozambique there are 80,000 **witch doctors** but only 350 conventional doctors. Traditional African medicine operates on principles which may seem strange

Homeopathy is one of the world's most popular types of CAM. More people proportionately use it in France than in any other country.

In India, Ayurvedic medicine is the only option for many people in poor families or rural areas. As well as being affordable, it has been used for thousands of years, and so is well known and trusted.

to Westerners, for example, the idea that disease may be caused by the spirits of angry ancestors. However, it works well for many illnesses, especially psychological ones, and uses many herbs now 'adopted' by Western CAM, such as African prune and aloe.

In Cuba, conventional medicines are running short. This is because the US government wants the country's Communist president, Fidel Castro, to be overthrown. It has not traded with Cuba for over 40 years, and punishes other countries which do so. Because of the lack of drugs, acupuncture is now often used to anaesthetize patients during surgery so they will feel no pain. The government is also collecting knowledge from elderly people about traditional herbal remedies, which are now sold in chemists' shops as *medicina verde* (green medicine).

Rabies in the Philippines

The deadly disease rabies is widespread in the Philippines. People bitten by dogs can go to their local health centre to have an injection to kill the virus before it reaches the brain. However, many people still rely – fatally – on cultural tradition, preferring to use *tandok* (healing stones), which they mistakenly believe can 'suck' out the virus. Even in countries where modern 'Western' medicine is available, it may be rejected because it is seen as foreign, and not part of the country's traditional culture.

Why is it used?

The general public today is better educated than ever before. Yet people are using more and more CAM treatments, many of which – according to medical researchers – have no basis in scientific fact. Why is this?

It could be partly due to people losing their faith in science, doctors and governments following a long history of health disasters and cover-ups. For example, there were huge problems with a drug called thalidomide. It was given to thousands of pregnant women in the 1960s to stop morning sickness. It turned out to cause terrible deformities in their babies.

Modern medicine often seems harsh. The **conventional** treatment for cancer is still to 'cut it (surgery), burn it (**radiotherapy**), then poison it (**chemotherapy**)', and many drugs have unpleasant **side effects**. For example, lithium, used to control the mood swings of people with **manic depression**, can also cause a person to shake uncontrollably.

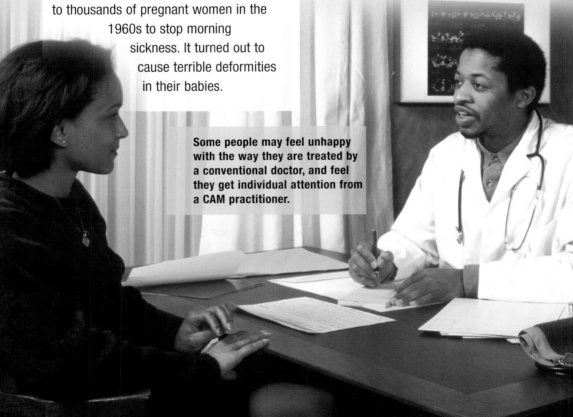

Some people may feel unhappy with the way they are treated by a conventional doctor, and feel they get individual attention from a CAM practitioner.

Simple principles

Alternative remedies are seen as gentler and safer. Instead of cold, rational science based on complicated hormones, antibodies, cells and genes, they operate on simple principles, such as preventing illness by getting the body's spirit and energy levels back into harmony.

Doctors in public healthcare systems are often too busy to spend more than a few minutes with each patient. Some say doctors do not take them seriously if they do not seem to have a 'real' medical problem, for example, if they just feel very tired or low. Alternative practitioners, meanwhile, usually spend up to an hour listening to patients' problems and firmly involve them in their own, individually tailored healing process.

Many CAM remedies can simply be bought over the counter in shops. They are often cheaper than prescription drugs, although therapies involving a visit to a practitioner's office can be quite expensive. A consultation with a homeopath in the USA costs the patient around $75.

While conventional medicine may offer only one or two drugs for each ailment, CAM provides a huge array which can be 'mixed and matched' until the patient finds one that suits him or her. In addition, new remedies, offering fresh hope, are being discovered all the time.

Although CAM medicines are generally gentler than their orthodox alternatives, care is needed during pregnancy. The unborn baby is very sensitive and can be damaged even by natural herbs and medicines.

Looking for miracles

CAM is often used by people suffering from life-threatening conditions such as cancer. In Western industrialized countries, cancer affects one person in three and kills one in five. Conventional treatments, such as **radiotherapy** and **chemotherapy**, sometimes extend sufferers' lives for only a few months anyway. When conventional treatments seem to offer little hope, desperate people often look for alternatives. In Australia, more than 50 per cent of cancer patients now use CAM, usually alongside **conventional medicine**. In the USA the figure may be as high as 75 per cent (see pages 38–9 on complementary cancer care).

The fight against toxins

Some of the therapies may seem quite extreme. One of the most popular alternative treatments for cancer is the Gerson diet. The theory is that the disease is caused by a build-up of **toxins** in the body. These can apparently be removed by consuming large amounts of fresh organic fruit and vegetables and taking vitamins. Several **enemas** using coffee are given each day. Essiac, a herb used by Native Americans, is another treatment claimed to be good at loosening up and expelling toxins from the body. Iscador, a popular treatment based on mistletoe, has shown tumour-fighting success in some studies.

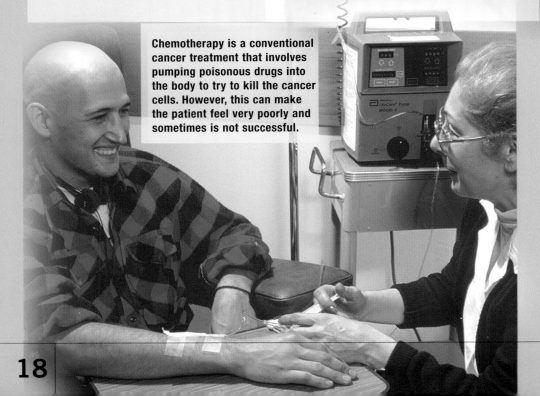

Chemotherapy is a conventional cancer treatment that involves pumping poisonous drugs into the body to try to kill the cancer cells. However, this can make the patient feel very poorly and sometimes is not successful.

Such treatments may have much to offer in some cases, but there is not yet enough evidence for them to be considered as miracle cures. If they were, then cancer would already have been wiped out.

Up to 30 per cent of cancers may be caused by poor nutrition. Most doctors agree that a more wholesome diet can be very important, especially in preventing cancer in the first place. However, people should never go on extreme diets without seeking their doctor's advice. It could make patients who are already very ill and weak much sicker.

Eating a lot of junk food, such as burgers and fries, may make people more likely to develop serious diseases such as cancer later in life.

Types and techniques

Millions of people in the Western world use the most popular CAM therapies – but how do they actually work?

- The theory behind **acupuncture** is that illness is caused by a disruption of **chi** (life energy), which runs through the body in invisible channels called **meridians**. This can cause problems at any point along the channel. For example, a blocked stomach meridian, which also runs through the gums, could cause toothache. To restore chi, **acupuncturists** insert thin needles into some of the 365 acupuncture points around the body. There is no pain, though patients may feel a slight tugging. Acupuncture can successfully treat conditions such as back pain, stress and nausea.

❝To say, as some therapists do, that there are many and equally valid maps of the body's workings is to say that there are many and equally valid road maps of London.❞

(John Diamond, British journalist who was doubtful about CAM, in *Snake Oil and Other Preoccupations*)

Flexible steel acupuncture needles are used to 'tap into' energy channels that practitioners believe to run through the body from the head to the feet.

- **Reflexology** works on similar principles as acupuncture, but with the hand or foot viewed as a smaller reflection of the body. Practitioners restore energy flow through **massage**.

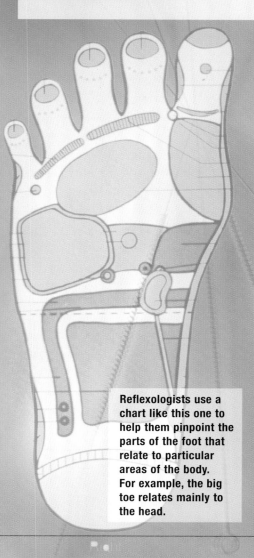

Reflexologists use a chart like this one to help them pinpoint the parts of the foot that relate to particular areas of the body. For example, the big toe relates mainly to the head.

- **Homeopathy** is based on the idea that 'like cures like'. For example, digoxin (from the foxglove flower) is a poison which can cause heart irregularities. It is used by homeopaths to cure heart problems. However, because homeopathic remedies are so heavily diluted (like a pinch of salt in the Atlantic Ocean), the liquid is said to contain only a 'memory' of the digoxin. The weaker the remedy, the greater its supposed ability to trigger the body's healing energy. A remedy may depend on the patient's **constitution** as well as the illness. A happy, outgoing person and a nervous, withdrawn person would receive different treatment for the same disease. Homeopathy is often used to treat allergies, asthma, eczema and anxiety. However, there is little accepted scientific evidence to show it actually works. Bach flower remedies are an offshoot of homeopathy. The 38 essences prepared from wild plants and rock water are used to affect a person's mood. One popular remedy is used to help people cope with stress, for example, before exams or after an argument.

Types and techniques

- In **herbal medicine**, plants and herbs are used to treat diseases and promote health. They are often broken down into four groups: tonics, specifics, heroics and cleansers. Tonics, such as ginseng, slowly and gently strengthen and nourish the body. They can be taken over long periods. Specifics are stronger, and are used temporarily to deal with a particular problem. For example, echinacea is used to prevent colds. Heroics are even stronger, and must be used under supervision. Cleansers, or protectors, remove poisons from the body. An example is pectin, which is found in apples and pears.

- Faith healing involves the healer calling on God, or on other forces such as the 'higher energy of the universe', to cure the patient. Healers may channel healing power through their hands. Some studies show that sick people who are prayed for recover quicker than others, but many people doubt these results.

- **Chiropractic** theory is that many health problems stem from bad positioning of the spine and the nerves that pass through it. Chiropractors adjust segments of the backbone using anything from very fast movements to deep massage. Chiropractic is used for back pain, migraine, asthma and sports injuries.

- **Hypnotherapy** was first practised in Ancient Egypt, where priests entered **hypnosis** through chanting. It was first popularized in the West by the Scottish doctor, James Braid, in the 1840s. The patient is sent into a **trance** – a deep state of relaxation – often by staring at a light or object, or listening to the therapist's voice. The person is still aware of his or her surroundings, but more affected by positive suggestions made by the therapist. Hypnotherapy may help people to give up smoking, overcome phobias (strong fears – for example of spiders) or become more self-confident.

Transcendental meditation

Many US companies, including car manufacturing giant General Motors, now offer **transcendental meditation** (TM) classes for their employees. Research has shown this can make people work more efficiently, take fewer sick days, feel happier in their jobs and get on better with fellow workers.

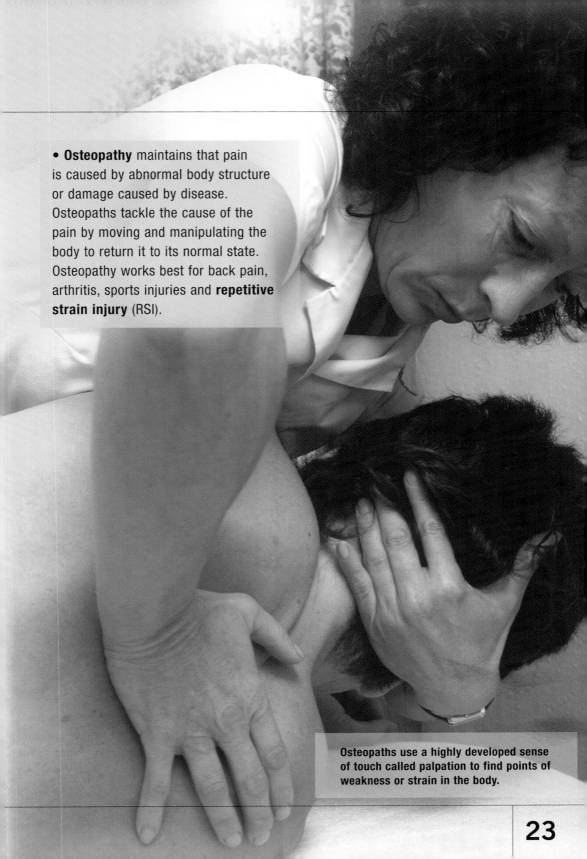

• **Osteopathy** maintains that pain is caused by abnormal body structure or damage caused by disease. Osteopaths tackle the cause of the pain by moving and manipulating the body to return it to its normal state. Osteopathy works best for back pain, arthritis, sports injuries and **repetitive strain injury** (RSI).

Osteopaths use a highly developed sense of touch called palpation to find points of weakness or strain in the body.

Types and techniques

- Massage stimulates the nerve endings in the skin, the body's largest sense organ. This reduces levels of stress-related chemicals in the body and generally promotes a feeling of well-being. Stronger massage relieves pain. There are various kinds, such as Swedish massage (using oils) and Japanese shiatsu, which stimulates pressure points.

- **Meditation** has been used for thousands of years in the East, but only became popular in the West in the 1960s after the British pop group, the Beatles, visited India. People who practise meditation say it is like taking a 'mental bath'. By concentrating on quiet, slow breathing they can calm the mind and reduce stress levels.

- Biofeedback is one of many popular relaxation techniques. Electronic devices attached to the body measure signals such as skin temperature, heart rate and brain waves. The device beeps when, for example, the person's muscles become too tense. The person learns to relax by consciously controlling the body's reactions to stress. It is said to be good for headaches, circulation problems and abnormal heartbeat. The Dallas Cowboys football team has used biofeedback to reduce stress and improve performance.

Fringe treatments

There are also many more forms of CAM. However, scientists and practitioners of the more 'respectable' therapies may doubt that these fringe treatments can work:

- Crystal healers believe the molecules (groups of atoms) in different types of crystals vibrate at different speeds. They choose the correct one to restore a sick patient's natural body vibrations to normal.

- Trepanation is the world's oldest form of surgery, dating back 7000 years. It involves drilling a hole in the patient's skull to allow better blood circulation around the brain.

- Fans of urine therapy drink, or even bathe in, their own urine. They say urine can help to build **immunity** – much like a vaccination – to conditions such as allergies, **diabetes** and **herpes**.

- Practitioners of the Russian Buteyko Method believe that many illnesses are caused by people breathing too deeply. They claim to cure these conditions by teaching people to breathe correctly.

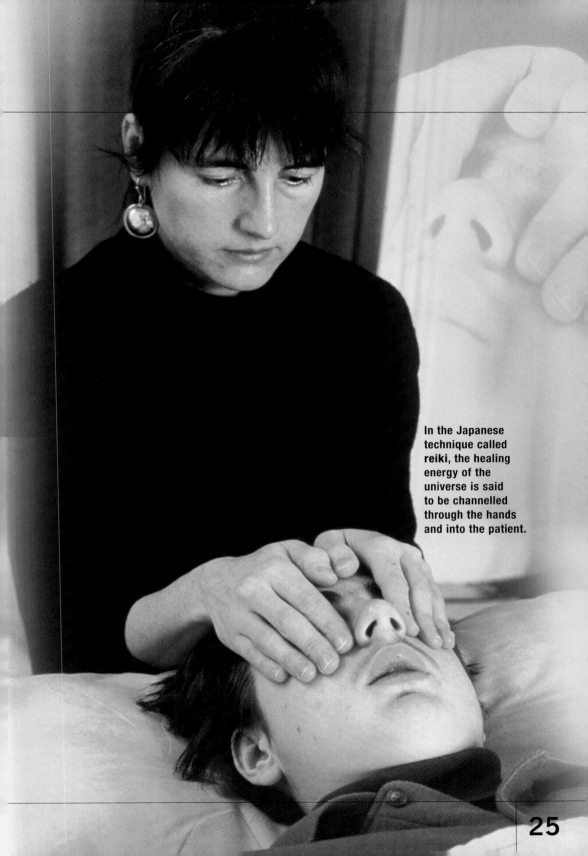

In the Japanese
technique called
reiki, the healing
energy of the
universe is said
to be channelled
through the hands
and into the patient.

Marijuana

Marijuana, or cannabis, is a controversial **alternative** therapy because in most places it is still an illegal drug. However, it has medical uses dating back thousands of years. In the nineteenth century, the British Queen Victoria used it for menstrual cramps. It was not actually banned in the USA until the 1920s.

Marijuana – the benefits

Marijuana's **active ingredient** is THC – tetra-hydrocannabinol. People with many serious diseases have found that it is often more helpful than prescribed drugs. For example, people with AIDS often become thin and malnourished, but find it hard to eat. They say that marijuana helps to stimulate their appetite. For people with cancer, it can help to reduce the sickness they often suffer while undergoing **chemotherapy** treatment.

Marijuana is also helpful for the eye condition glaucoma. It can lower internal eye pressure associated with the disease, slowing the onset of blindness. It also seems to calm pain and muscle seizures among sufferers of **multiple sclerosis**, epilepsy and spinal cord injuries.

Research into the benefits of marijuana is now progressing rapidly in many countries. In the UK, for example, there is a big ongoing trial involving multiple sclerosis patients. If proved effective, marijuana could be available on prescription by 2004. Nevertheless, at the moment, sufferers (or their families or friends) in many countries still have to buy the drug illegally. They risk fines or imprisonment.

The medical form of marijuana is much weaker than the kind smoked by drug-users to obtain a 'high'. It is hoped this will cut down on rare **side effects** such as hallucinations (seeing or hearing things which are not there) and paranoia (fear that other people hate you or are ganging up on you).

The downside

Some studies have shown that marijuana may cause cancer and increase the risk of heart disease. This is not important for people who are terminally ill and simply want to relieve their pain. Yet anti-drug campaigners say more research is needed before medical marijuana use should be allowed. They say that tighter rules are needed to prevent the law being exploited by illegal drug abusers.

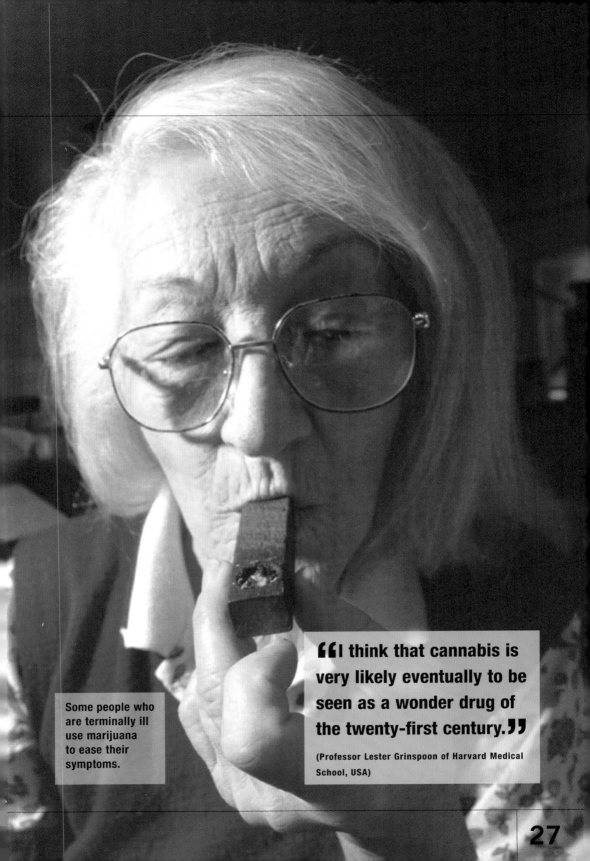

Some people who are terminally ill use marijuana to ease their symptoms.

❝I think that cannabis is very likely eventually to be seen as a wonder drug of the twenty-first century.❞

(Professor Lester Grinspoon of Harvard Medical School, USA)

Naturopathy

Naturopathy is a kind of 'catch-all' treatment, which brings together many of the major **alternative** treatments. Hippocrates, the Ancient Greek physician known as the 'father of medicine', laid the foundations for it 2500 years ago. He said that health could be maintained by the correct balance of sleep, exercise and plain food. This idea was further developed at Austrian and German health spas in the nineteenth century and by the health-conscious US breakfast cereal manufacturer, John Kellogg.

medicines are not used to suppress, or hide, these symptoms. Treatments are aimed at restoring the patient's 'vital force' to a point where his or her body can heal itself.

Rather like **Ayurveda** (see page 12), naturopathic medicine relies on a wide range of treatments, including **detoxifying diets**, exercise, herbs, **yoga**, **osteopathy**, **homeopathy**, hydrotherapy (hot and cold baths and steam treatment), **massage** and **acupuncture**.

A matter of lifestyle

Naturopaths believe more in building long-term health than fighting disease. This means naturopathy often involves a whole change of lifestyle, rather than being something to be used as a 'quick fix' if people feel poorly.

Naturopathy emphasizes the 'natural' in the belief that the body can be weakened by bad diet, pollution, stress or the lack of fresh air. Symptoms of disease are seen as signs of the body working to heal itself, and so

Taking regular exercise is a good way of boosting immunity and preventing illness.

Patterns or blotches on the iris of the eye may be a sign of problems elsewhere in the body.

Iridology and applied kinesiology

Some naturopaths use iridology. This involves examining the iris, the coloured part of the eye. Like fingerprints, all irises are different, and changes in the iris's pattern are thought to give information about problems inside the body. Applied kinesiology is sometimes used to diagnose allergies. The patient is asked to hold one arm out at right angles to the body, and the therapist attempts to push it back into place, judging the patient's muscle strength. The exercise is then repeated, with the patient holding a potential allergen – for example wheat – in the other hand. If the person is allergic to wheat, it should be easier to push the arm down, because an allergy-causing substance is supposed to affect a person's energy. No research evidence to support these techniques exists yet.

The role of the media

CAM remedies are regularly featured in news reports and advertisements in top magazines or on prime-time television. Sales of CAM products usually shoot up following reports about therapies. This is especially the case if they are linked to a high profile celebrity, for example 'Friends' star Jennifer Aniston, who used **hypnotherapy** to give up smoking, or Guns 'n' Roses singer Axl Rose, who is a big fan of **homeopathy**.

The media are important in broadening our knowledge of CAM. Most people first learn about new therapies and products – what they are good for, how to use them, and where to find them – from newspapers and the television.

'Miracle cure' stories

However, it is important to keep an open mind. CAM therapies may be called 'wonder cures'. But if you read carefully, many of these stories are only about plans to conduct trials on the therapy. It is hoped it may turn out to be a wonder cure but nothing has yet been proved. **Conventional medicine**, meanwhile, is governed by much stricter reporting regulations.

The big companies which fund medical research do not allow scientists to talk about possible new drugs until all the results have been gathered in. This can take a very long time. Therefore it can sometimes seem that modern medicine has less to offer than CAM. The media want big, dramatic stories about disasters, scandals and miraculous medicines. Headlines such as: 'Cancer – scientists still working on cure' do not sell newspapers.

Many health professionals worry about media reports of unusual cases, for example of people 'beating' cancer with CAM. They fear this could even encourage people to abandon conventional treatment. CAM does seem to work well for some conditions in some circumstances. It will almost definitely turn out to have even more benefits when properly studied. However, despite hundreds of hopeful 'miracle cure' stories, research has not yet shown clearly that any CAM remedy can treat cancer or prevent diseases such as measles and smallpox as effectively as modern medicine and mass **immunization** programmes.

Like many other
Hollywood stars,
Jennifer Aniston has
used CAM therapies.

❝Migraine headaches are really terrible. I tried a homeopathic remedy, and all I can say is 'Wow!' – what a blessing!❞

(Demetrios Vouganis of Sandy, Utah quoted on a website)

Does it work?

With billions of dollars spent each year on CAM, why are there still so many arguments about whether or not it actually works? One reason is that many CAM treatments are taken daily over many years to slowly improve health rather than to quickly cure a specific illness.

On top of this, there are many factors involved in sickness and recovery, and the body sometimes works in ways scientists cannot explain. For example, a few cancers go into **remission** (disappear) for no obvious reason. Someone who had followed the Gerson diet might be convinced he or she had been cured by CAM. This is possible but unlikely – because many people using such therapies do not recover.

Proving they work

The biggest problem is that it has not yet been possible to test many CAM remedies and show they work as well as prescription drugs. An exception is the herb St John's Wort, used for treating mild depression. In Germany it outsells the anti-depressant drug Prozac by 12:1.

Some therapies also claim to operate on such unusual principles that it is difficult to 'prove' them in laboratory experiments. Homeopathic remedies, for example, have often been shown to contain nothing but water and alcohol. And there is no sign of the energy channels which **acupuncturists** claim run through the body.

However, **homeopathy** and **acupuncture** do seem to work for some conditions. A possible explanation is that acupuncture actually taps into nerves, switching off pain signals in the brain. The repeated shaking involved in the preparation of homeopathic remedies might somehow change the structure of water molecules.

In any case, the failure to show clear results may not necessarily mean a product does not work. Even tests into widely accepted **conventional** drugs can have conflicting results. Some big tests on Prozac, for example, have 'proved' it works well for 80 per cent of depression sufferers. Others show it has hardly any effect.

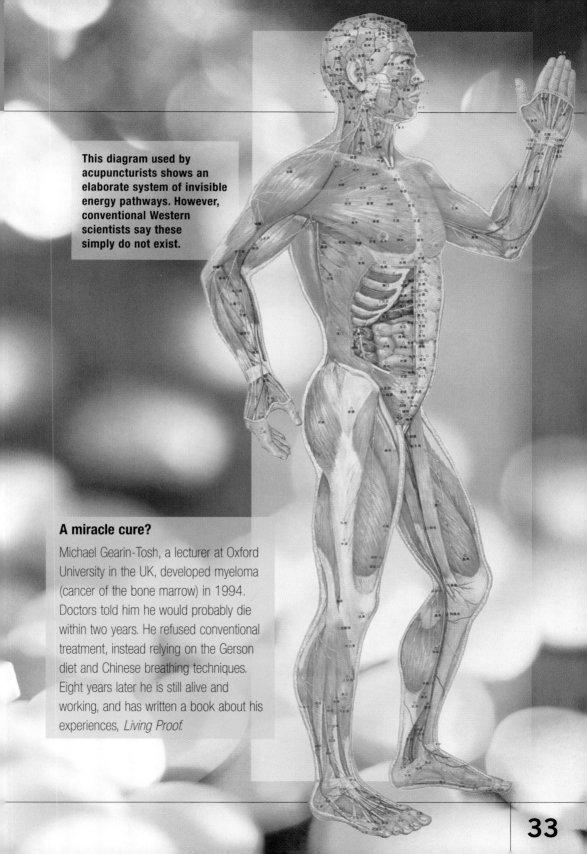

This diagram used by acupuncturists shows an elaborate system of invisible energy pathways. However, conventional Western scientists say these simply do not exist.

A miracle cure?

Michael Gearin-Tosh, a lecturer at Oxford University in the UK, developed myeloma (cancer of the bone marrow) in 1994. Doctors told him he would probably die within two years. He refused conventional treatment, instead relying on the Gerson diet and Chinese breathing techniques. Eight years later he is still alive and working, and has written a book about his experiences, *Living Proof*.

All in the mind?

Did you know that the human brain can produce pain-killing chemicals as powerful as anything made in a laboratory? People who have suffered terrible injuries in wars and disasters sometimes do not even realize until some time later. Some people have even lost a limb, for example after being shot or attacked by a shark – but felt no pain.

The powerful brain

Yoga experts can consciously alter body functions such as their heartbeat or temperature. Many people who are allergic to **anaesthetics** can go through surgery after being hypnotized and feel little or no pain. Many CAM therapies, such as **massage** and **meditation**, trigger the brain to release small amounts of pain-killing, 'feel-good' chemicals, called endorphins. One study on the effects of **reflexology** even found changes in the brains of rats after they had had their paws massaged.

The brain clearly works in powerful ways, which scientists admit they are still far from understanding. This may help to explain why some supposedly 'medically impossible' alternative therapies seem to work so well, at least in some patients.

The placebo effect

A scientific phenomenon known as the **placebo effect** exists. More than 30 per cent of sick people will improve if given a treatment by a doctor – even if the treatment actually contains no medicine at all. If people believe they are going to get better, their brains can sometimes actually suppress their symptoms or boost their immune system to fight off the illness. However, placebo-induced effects, unlike a genuine cure, rarely last long. Most patients quickly return to their original condition.

Positive thinking

Dr Dean Ornish, a charming and confident doctor in the USA, reported a large fall in heart disease among patients who followed his strict regime of diet, positive thinking and meditation. In 2002, similar improvements were noted at eight other test sites in the country. However, the major organizations working with heart conditions in the USA did not accept that it was possible to reverse heart disease.

The aim of meditation is to relax and clear the mind. When done properly, it seems to improve people's health and could even increase their life expectancy.

The benefits

Many conventional doctors now use CAM to treat patients for some conditions. Why do they do this? Many doctors have seen for themselves that CAM – even if it has not been scientifically proven – sometimes works better for their patients than prescription drugs. In fact, most family doctors' surgeries, pain clinics and **hospices** offer a range of the better-established therapies, such as **acupuncture**, **homeopathy** and **massage**.

Psychological problems

Many of the common conditions for which doctors prescribe CAM have a psychological aspect – to do with a person's mind and emotions. One in four people in Western countries suffer from depression at some point in their lives. Many others are hit by anxiety, stress at work and panic attacks. If untreated, these can go on to become the root of other common complaints, such as migraines, high blood pressure, unexplained pains and digestive problems.

Because CAM works holistically, it is often much better than **conventional medicine** at dealing with all the underlying causes of a problem. As the **placebo effect** shows, the mind has a great deal of control over the body's healing processes. Unlike busy doctors, practitioners spend a long time talking to their patients, and help them to unlock their own healing powers. This can be much more successful than a doctor's pills for people whose problems stem from depression or stress.

Physical problems

CAM works well for many purely physical complaints too. More and more people now do little exercise and work in front of a computer all day. Back pain, **repetitive strain injury** and other physical problems are becoming more common. Massage, acupuncture and **osteopathy** can often treat these more successfully than painkillers.

Work-related stress is a problem that affects nearly everybody at some time or another. If untreated, it can go on to cause a wide range of physical problems.

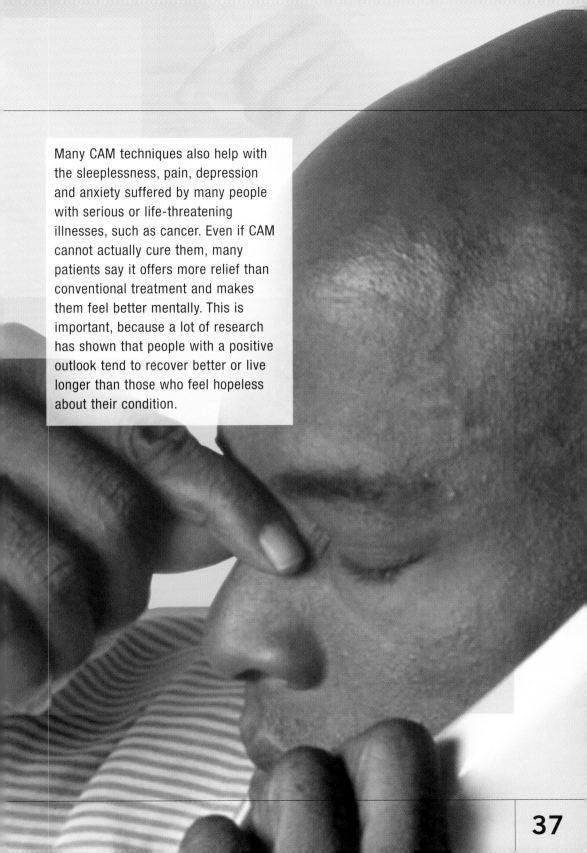

Many CAM techniques also help with the sleeplessness, pain, depression and anxiety suffered by many people with serious or life-threatening illnesses, such as cancer. Even if CAM cannot actually cure them, many patients say it offers more relief than conventional treatment and makes them feel better mentally. This is important, because a lot of research has shown that people with a positive outlook tend to recover better or live longer than those who feel hopeless about their condition.

Curing body and spirit

The relationship between **conventional** and **alternative medicine** has traditionally been hostile. Several years ago, the British Medical Journal described **chiropractic** as no more useful than the 'examination of a bird's entrails'. (Ancient peoples thought they could foretell the future by looking at the innards of dead animals.) But things are changing. Today, most CAM is actually used in a complementary way, alongside conventional medicine. For example, a person may use **homeopathy** to calm his or her nerves before surgery.

Mind, body and spirit

Doctors now increasingly realize that many patients want and need treatment for their 'spirit' as well as their body. Conventional medicine usually does not provide this emotional and spiritual backup. Many doctors therefore now accept CAM techniques as long as they do not compete with or replace conventional treatment. At least 40 per cent of general medicine surgeries in Europe, and even more **hospices** and pain clinics, now offer complementary therapies to help increase the success of a patient's treatment.

Traditional healing

In the USA, successful programmes for treating alcoholism among Native Americans mix psychiatric counselling with traditional healing arts. These include chanting, 'smudging' (burning sage or scented woods), sweat lodges (see page 46) and dream interpretation. The drug peyote is used, which makes people hallucinate (see things that are not there).

The Bristol Cancer Help Centre

The Bristol Cancer Help Centre, in the UK, has been a pioneer in this area. The centre's philosophy is that each person's 'journey with cancer' is unique. The World Health Organization says it represents 'the gold standard for complementary care in cancer'. Alongside the patient's conventional treatment programme, staff devise an individual plan of relaxation, **meditation**, **visualization**, music or art therapy, spiritual healing and **massage**. These are called psycho neuro immunology (PNI) therapies. The staff work together with the patient's surgeons to make sure no therapy will interfere with their medical treatment.

Many studies have shown that these therapies can greatly improve on conventional treatment alone. They may help create natural killer cells in the body, which destroy unhealthy cancer cells. People who have received PNI treatment certainly tend to be happier and more relaxed, live longer, cope better with the trauma of having a life-threatening illness, and recover better from treatments such as **chemotherapy**.

The Bristol Cancer Help Centre looks after every aspect of a patient's needs. It provides peaceful gardens where people can relax and quality meals packed full of healthy ingredients to help sick people to get better.

The dangers

Around 130,000 Americans die each year from the **side effects** of prescription drugs. CAM products are generally much safer. However, nothing is risk-free. Kava kava, a herb used to treat anxiety, has been linked to liver failure. Gingko biloba (used to boost brain power) and echinacea (to prevent colds) could reduce fertility.

The quality of herbs

A problem is that the quality of herbs can vary a lot, depending on the soil in which they were grown, the climate, and how they are stored. In 1998, the *Los Angeles Times* tested ten popular brands of St John's Wort. Three had less than half the strength listed on the label. **Complementary medicines** may also interact with **conventional** ones in dangerous ways. St John's Wort, garlic and gingko biloba can stop blood-thinning drugs working properly. St John's Wort may also affect the contraceptive pill and medicines for asthma, epilepsy and migraine. Some products might be contaminated too. Lead, arsenic and mercury were found in one-third of Asian herbals tested in California in 1998.

Dangerous practices

Although most people in the West get enough vitamins from their diet, some people take mega-doses for their supposed health benefits. Occasionally they end up poisoning themselves. Children are at greatest risk of overdose, because their bodies are smaller. Even therapies that do not involve swallowing products are not 100 per cent safe. For example, **hypnotherapy** could be dangerous for the depressed or epileptic.

However, the biggest danger is not from using CAM therapies, but from not using conventional treatment. For example, relying on faith healing alone can be very dangerous. There have been many cases of people dying from easily curable diseases after refusing conventional medical treatment. In 1996, several children in Germany died after homeopaths told their parents to stop giving them insulin for **diabetes**. This condition can be kept under control with conventional drugs. The homeopathic remedies were themselves harmless, but the 'treatment' killed them.

Garlic – the pros and cons

Garlic is often taken by HIV sufferers to stop the build-up of **cholesterol** that is caused by their medication. In 2001, researchers at the US National Institutes of Health found that garlic had the unwanted **side effect** of massively reducing the levels of important anti-HIV drugs in their blood.

Healers or fakers?

Many CAM practitioners, for example osteopaths and Chinese herbalists, study for a long time at university. Yet others can train in just a couple of months and may have very little medical knowledge. In a British trial of reflexologists in 2000, not one could diagnose six common illnesses when they were stopped from actually talking to the patients.

Tapping into fears

Unfortunately, not all people selling CAM products are what they seem. Some take advantage of sick or frightened people, selling them useless 'remedies' to get rich quick. Within days of the terrorist attacks of 11 September 2001 in the USA, 200 websites sprang up claiming their **herbal** remedies could cure anthrax. At the time it was feared terrorists might release the germs causing this very infectious disease to kill thousands of people. However, anthrax can kill in days – much too fast for oregano oil or zinc water to work. The only known treatment is very strong **antibiotics**.

Operation Cure All

The US Federal Trade Commission launched 'Operation Cure All' in 1997 to crack down on Internet companies making such false claims. However, the Internet is hard to police, so anyone surfing the Net should be wary. Warning bells should ring if a product claims to be a panacea, or cure-all, capable of clearing up anything from baldness to heart disease. Panaceas do not exist. Also worrying are products that claim to have 'secret ingredients', or adverts that include the amazing success stories of unnamed patients. These are easy to invent. Health frauds also often talk of secret government plots to suppress their miracle cure.

❝Your very first capsule will start to melt down fat just like hot water melts down ice!❞

(Claim made by the manufacturers of an alternative weight loss pill – despite this being a physical impossibility)

Therapeutic Touch

In 1998, Colorado schoolgirl Emily Rosa caused huge embarrassment to practitioners of Therapeutic Touch (TT), who claim to sense and heal the human 'energy field'. In an experiment, she showed they could not sense anything at all when a barrier stopped them from seeing if a patient was actually in front of them. The practitioners complained Emily had blocked their powers with her 'negative energy'. The American magician, James Randi, has offered one million dollars to anyone who can prove that TT actually works. So far, no one has been able to do so.

It is important to be careful when using the Internet to find out about CAM treatments. Information may seem convincing but could be misleading or even completely wrong.

Radionics

One dubious CAM 'therapy' is radionics. Practitioners claim to use psychic powers and a mysterious 'black box' to heal the sick and advise on gambling and animal breeding – sometimes from hundreds of miles away. US practitioner, Shelvie Rettman, was convicted of fraud in 1998 after advising a cancer patient to stop **chemotherapy**. The patient, who was charged $2,000 for 'treatment', died soon afterwards.

The need for research

Despite their popularity, 'the jury is still out' on CAM products, simply because few have been tested in the kind of trials which mainstream drugs must undergo to prove that they work. In fact, most good practitioners would like their therapy to be properly tested. Then everyone could see, once and for all, that it is effective. However, many manufacturers are small firms lacking enough money to do such testing.

Pharma companies

Big **pharmaceutical** companies are usually not interested in testing CAM, as natural products cannot have a **patent** taken out on them. In fact, some CAM manufacturers believe the big drug companies are actively blocking research. Natural alternatives – if scientifically proven – could pose dangerous competition to their chemical products. There has traditionally been little interest from governments either. They have not been keen to spend taxpayers' money on researching remedies unlikely to be dramatically effective.

Government research

However, with at least one in five people in Western countries using CAM, this situation benefits only the fraudsters, who get rich from patients' ignorance. Some much-needed research is now finally being done. The budget of the US government's National Center for Complementary and Alternative Medicine (NCCAM) rose from $2 million in 1993 to almost $70 million in 2000. Australia has a Complementary Medicines Evaluation Committee (CMEC). In Canada, the government set up an Office of Natural Health Products in 1999. It is working to ensure the safety of CAM products.

Yet the amount spent on researching CAM is a tiny fraction of the amount spent on conventional medical research. In the UK, for example, the Department of Health in 2002 spent only 0.08 per cent of its annual research budget on CAM. To prove their worth in tests, CAM products must show they work better than a **placebo** and have no dangerous **side effects**. Large trials involving hundreds of people are needed, not just individual success stories.

"A potentially powerful resource is at our fingertips, but its benefits will be limited...unless somewhere, somehow, purses are opened and funds dedicated to its systematic study."

(Britain's Prince Charles, who in 2000 tried to persuade the UK government to spend £10 million on a five-year CAM research programme)

Herbs and the environment

We now use more than 700 **herbal** remedies. The raw products for some, such as St John's Wort, are grown and harvested at massive farms. Yet up to 90 per cent are still harvested from the wild. Many people mistakenly think wild herbs are better than farmed herbs. This has led to many popular European and North American herb species, including arnica and echinacea, becoming endangered through over-collection.

Although licenses are now needed to harvest many European and North American herbs, many in the developing world are still threatened – often by loss of habitat. Nearly one-third of all our medicines come from plants. Scientists believe we are most likely to find cures for cancer and AIDS in the millions of plants in the world's tropical rainforests. However, without protection, the last rainforests could disappear by the year 2015.

Ethno-medicine

There could also be great potential, for both **conventional medicine** and CAM, in ethno-medicine. This comes from traditional remedies used by people of the world's remote mountains, jungles and deserts. In fact, many of today's CAM treatments have been 'discovered' in this way. **Reiki**, for example, was developed by a Japanese man, who based it on ancient Tibetan traditions. Practitioners use their hands to channel healing reiki ('universal energy' in Japanese) into the patient's body.

Meanwhile Native American sweat lodges have become popular in many parts of the USA. Hot and steamy, they are used to cleanse the skin, calm the mind and keep disease at bay. Western doctors nowadays also often advise 'flu patients to breathe in steam to kill bugs in their lungs.

With so many diseases which still cannot be fully cured, we could learn a lot by studying techniques which have been used by people around the world over thousands of years.

Indigenous peoples around the world often have their own ways of treating diseases. Some of these may turn out to work better than the methods used in the West today.

Oils for aches and pains

Australian aborigines have always used tea tree oil. Trials in 1923 showed it was a good antiseptic, so it was issued to Australian soldiers in World War Two. The white settlers also borrowed the Aborigines' Goanna Oil, a mixture of eucalyptus, pine, mint and menthol used for aches and pains. (The traditional recipe also includes skink – a type of lizard.) Today, scientists are asking the Aborigines about many of their other traditional remedies in the hope of discovering other useful medicines.

Legal matters

Manufacturers of medical drugs are governed by strict regulations. However, few types of CAM are classed as medicines because they have not been proved in clinical trials accepted by government scientists. In the USA, therefore, herbs are seen as food supplements and do not have to be screened by the Federal Drug Administration (FDA) to prove they are safe.

Fair trade rules

In fact, the only laws governing many CAM products are fair trade rules about making false claims – the same as those applied to used car salesmen. There is evidence, for example, that St John's Wort may work as well as **conventional medicines** to help fight depression. Yet the label on the bottle can only say: 'Helps support a positive mood.'

Regulation

The regulation of practitioners in the USA varies from state to state. Naturopaths are licensed in 11 states, **acupuncturists** in 34 and chiropractors in all 50. In Canada only licensed physicians may practise **homeopathy**. In Australia, the National Herbalists Association of Australia (NHAA) was founded in 1920 to maintain minimum standards. There are twelve colleges teaching the subject. To ensure quality and safety, the government has set up a Complementary Medicines Evaluation Committee.

In the UK, there is little regulation at all. Anyone can set him or herself up as a practitioner so long as they do not practise dentistry, deliver babies, treat sexually transmitted diseases or work as vets. However, osteopaths and chiropractors must now be trained and qualified to a minimum standard.

These students of reflexology will spend several years learning how to treat people. Yet others may learn in just a few weeks. This is hardly enough time to cover the basics, and they may end up doing more harm than good.

The Department of Health will soon also start regulating **acupuncture**, **herbal medicine** and possibly some other therapies. In most other European countries, only medical doctors can offer CAM and they must have a government licence. Germany has thousands of *Heilpraktiker* (naturopathic healers), licensed as long as they pass a test in basic medical knowledge. Most legitimate practitioners want to be regulated, because it means they can control the prices of treatment and provide a good standard of service.

Marijuana

In 2001, Canada became the first country to decriminalize marijuana for medical use, meaning people could use it if they were very ill. Patients, who need a photo identity card and permission from their doctor, can either grow their own or buy it from government-licensed farms. Some US states, such as California, have also legalized medical marijuana. However, possessing it is still illegal under federal law. Patients could, in theory, be prosecuted.

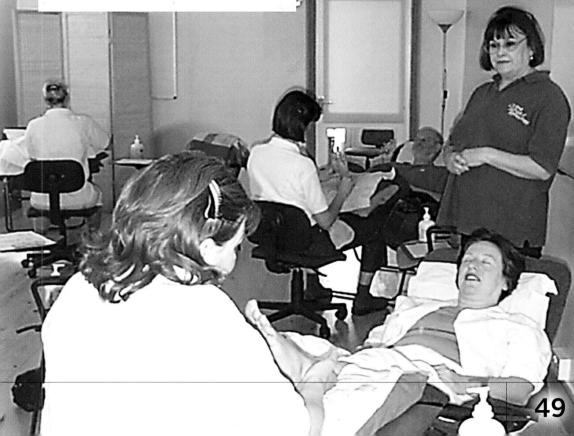

People to talk to

In the world of CAM, it can sometimes be difficult to tell the fraudsters from good practitioners, to know how much to pay, or how to make sense of the huge range of information available.

Books and websites

It is important to listen to both sides of the debate. Information in books written by experts is likely to be more reliable than information on unofficial Internet sites. The best books may be those written by medical doctors, or which state that they have been 'peer reviewed'. This means the facts or research have been checked and approved by health professionals.

Doctors

A good doctor will know about the potential risks and **side effects** of the more common CAM techniques. Some doctors may be very 'anti' CAM, or may not know a great deal about a specific therapy. In this case, a patient may choose another doctor who is more open-minded. However, it is always vital to get a medical diagnosis before deciding whether CAM is appropriate. A doctor should be kept informed of any CAM therapies a patient is using.

Practitioners

Practitioners can give detailed information about their particular therapy. However, many therapists do not have to meet the same minimum standards as doctors. It is a good idea to check out their qualifications, years of experience, whether they are licensed, and get information from them in writing. A good practitioner will not suggest the wrong treatment or advise avoiding **conventional medicine** for serious conditions.

Other organizations

Many people find it useful to talk to a charity or organization related to their disease or health condition. These often have the most up-to-date information on research and good CAM alternatives to conventional medicine. Government offices dealing with natural remedies or fair trade offices can give advice about products which are potentially dangerous, or have been banned. They will know about practitioners who have had legal action taken against them. Pharmacists can help explain the level of **active ingredients** in herbs and vitamins, and whether these are strong enough to have any effect.

It is often useful to speak to other people who have used the practitioner or therapy, and find out about their experiences. National professional organizations devoted to the therapy in question are also usually able to provide lists of the best practitioners.

Information and advice

The following organizations, groups, websites and books can provide a huge amount of information and advice on CAM, from all sides of the debate.

www.plantsavers.org
Information about endangered medicinal plants.

www.paston.co.uk/users/webbooks/chronol.html
Links to articles from all over the world explaining the history of medical cannabis and the latest developments in the campaign to legalize it.

www.hon.ch
The Health on the Net Foundation gives reliable medical information and expertise.

Contacts in the UK

British Complementary Medicine Association
PO Box 2074, Seaford, BN25 1HQ, Sussex
Tel: 0845 3455977
www.bcma.co.uk

British Holistic Medical Association
59 Lansdowne Place, Hove, BN3 1FL, Sussex Tel: 01273 725951
www.bhma.org

British Homeopathic Association
15 Clerkenwell Close, London, EC1R 0AA
Tel: 020 7566 7800
www.trusthomeopathy.org

Dr Edward Bach Centre
Mount Vernon, Bakers Lane, Sotwell, Oxon, OX10 0PZ Tel: 01491 834678
www.bachcentre.com

Contacts in the USA

The Alternative Medicine Foundation
www.amfoundation.org
Information on therapies and practitioners.

The Foundation for the Advancement of Innovative Medicine www.faim.org

National Center for Complementary and Alternative Medicine (NCCAM) at the National Institutes of Health (NIH)
www.nccam.nih.gov

National Council Against Health Fraud
www.ncahf.org

www.healthwatcher.net/Quackerywatch/Alternative-medicine
Information on health scams and quacks in the USA and Canada.

www.rxmarihuana.com
This site has a question and answer section about medical marijuana hosted by professors from Harvard Medical School.

Contacts in Canada

www.hc-sc.gc.ca/english/
Health Care Canada online.

www.canadian-health-network.ca and **www.canadianwellness.com/alternative/alternative.asp**
Sites with articles and advice about CAM use and tips for choosing a practitioner.

Contacts in Australia

Australian Government Health Department
www.health.gov.au

Australian Medical Association
www.ama.com.au

www.gemstate.net/Susan/linksAMed.htm
This huge site has information and links to therapies, literature and practitioners.

Contact in New Zealand

www.piperpat.co.nz/nz/alternat.html
A vast encyclopedia of the CAM therapies on offer and contact details for practitioners around the country.

Further reading

Alternative Medicine: Is It For You?
(Issues in Focus) by Kathiann M. Kowalski; Enslow Publishers, Inc., 1998.
A book aimed at student readers with detailed chapters on many different therapies, how they developed and the current state of research in alternative medicine.

Alternative Medicine: What Works, by Adriane Fugh-Berman; Lippincott Williams and Wilkins, 1997.
An easy-to-read review of the scientific evidence for CAM, written by a medical doctor and explaining scientific terms and types of research.

The Complete Guide: Integrated Medicine, by Dr David Peters and Anne Woodham; Dorling Kindersley, 2000.
Practical information on 40 conditions, from colds to cancer, that doctors believe benefit most from integrating complementary therapies with the best of medical science.

The Encyclopedia of Medicinal Plants, by Andrew Chevallier; Dorling Kindersley, 1998.
A fully illustrated guide to 550 medicinal plants, their therapeutic uses and the history of herbal medicine.

Smart Medicine for a Healthier Child: A Practical A–Z Reference to Natural and Conventional Treatments for Children and Infants, by Janet Zand, Rachel Walton, Robert Rountree and Bob Rountree; Avery Publishing Group, 1994.
Looks at both the alternative and conventional treatments for most common medical conditions.

Snake Oil and Other Preoccupations, by John Diamond; Vintage, 2001.
A book undermining quackery and therapies which give false hope to the seriously ill, written by a famous British journalist who died of cancer.

Glossary

active ingredients
ingredients in a medicine that act on the body

acupuncturist
a person who practises **acupuncture** – healing by placing needles at certain points in the body

alternative medicine
medicine that is not scientifically proven

anaesthetic
a drug given to make a person go numb in a certain part of the body, or go into a deep sleep

antibiotics
medicines that can destroy or prevent the growth of bacteria and cure infections

Ayurveda
an ancient Indian medical system based on the idea that illness is caused by an imbalance of the different types of energy in the body

chemotherapy
chemicals given to cancer patients to help kill cancer cells

chi
life energy, which some CAM practitioners believe runs through the body in channels

chiropractic
a treatment in which the spine is adjusted to help to cure health problems

cholesterol
type of fat that can build up inside blood vessels due to a fatty diet and little exercise

complementary medicine
medicine that is used alongside conventional medicine to treat aspects of an illness that conventional medicine may not be able to deal with easily

constitution
the description of a person according to their physical and personality type

conventional medicine
medicine practised by most doctors and hospitals in the Western world; also known as orthodox medicine

detoxifying diet
a diet for flushing out toxins, or poisons, from the body

diabetes
a disease that makes people unable to break down sugar in their bodies; many diabetics have to inject a hormone called insulin each day

enema
liquid forced into someone's anus (bottom) through a hose to clean out his or her intestines

herbal medicine
the use of herbs and plants to treat diseases and promote health

herpes
a virus that can cause cold sores on the lips

holistic treatment
treatment for the whole person rather than just the symptoms of the illness

homeopathy
treatment based on using tiny amounts of natural products to promote healing in the body

hospice
a special hospital for terminally ill people

hypnosis
a state of deep relaxation in which a person can still see and hear and follow commands

hypnotherapy
a treatment involving hypnosis to treat a patient

immunity
the body's ability to fight off infections and diseases. **Immunization** makes people immune to a disease, usually through an injection.

manic depression (bipolar affective disorder)
a disorder which causes huge mood swings, from feeling extremely happy to very low

massage
rubbing and pressing a person's body to reduce muscle and joint pain, and improve overall physical and mental health

meditation
an ancient Eastern practice: people concentrate on a word, a light or an idea and clear their minds to focus on their breathing

meridians
invisible energy channels which acupuncturists believe to run through the body

multiple sclerosis
a disease of the nervous system that can cause muscle stiffness, shaking, pain and tiredness

naturopathy
a way of building up health and energy through diet, exercise and a healthy lifestyle

orthodox medicine
(see conventional medicine)

osteopathy
the treatment of illness and pain by pressing and moving the bones and muscles

patent
the official right to control and receive income from an invention

pharmaceutical
to do with making and selling drugs

placebo effect
when people's symptoms disappear after receiving treatment that contains no medication

radiotherapy
radiation therapy given to cancer patients to reduce the size of their tumours

reflexology
a system of massage of the hand or foot used to relieve tension and treat illness

reiki
a type of healing in which the practitioner channels healing energy into the patient's body

remission
a stage where a cancerous tumour or other disorder seems to disappear or stop growing or spreading. If a patient is in remission for five years, he or she is said to be cured.

repetitive strain injury
a type of injury common in people who strain their muscles by making the same movements for long periods

side effects
an extra, and usually bad, effect of a drug

toxins
poisonous substances taken in by the body, for example from smoking or eating vegetables treated with pesticides

trance
a state of very deep relaxation into which someone enters during hypnotherapy

transcendental meditation
a method of detaching oneself from problems by meditating and chanting

visualization
the use of special meditation techniques, for example, picturing a tumour getting smaller

witch doctor
a traditional medicine man who often combines magical practices with alternative medicine

yoga
a system of body and breathing exercises used for relaxation and the development of strength and flexibility

Index

Titles in the *Need to Know* series include:

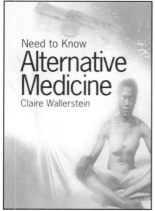

Need to Know
Alternative Medicine
Claire Wallerstein

Hardback   0 431 09808 5

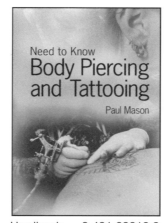

Need to Know
Body Piercing and Tattooing
Paul Mason

Hardback   0 431 09818 2

Need to Know
Depression
Claire Wallerstein

Hardback   0 431 09809 3

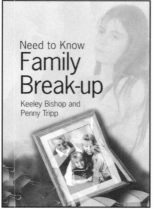

Need to Know
Family Break-up
Keeley Bishop and Penny Tripp

Hardback   0 431 09810 7

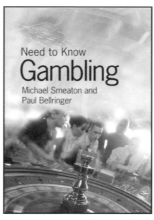

Need to Know
Gambling
Michael Smeaton and Paul Bellringer

Hardback   0 431 09819 0

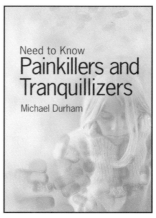

Need to Know
Painkillers and Tranquillizers
Michael Durham

Hardback   0 431 09811 5

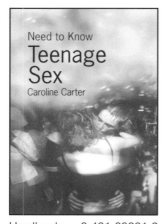

Need to Know
Teenage Sex
Caroline Carter

Hardback   0 431 09821 2

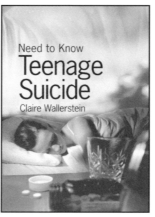

Need to Know
Teenage Suicide
Claire Wallerstein

Hardback   0 431 09820 4

Find out about the other titles in this series on our website www.heinemann.co.uk/library